Phl

Jennifer Harme

G000047770

Front cover: *Phlox paniculata* 'Monica Lynden-Bell

Parts 1 and 4 by Jennifer Harmer; Parts 2 and 3 by Dr Jack Elliott

All drawings, including the front cover, by Sue Ward

Edited and typeset by George Parker

Consultant editor to the Booklet Series: Tony Lord

© The Hardy Plant Society – October 2001

ISBN 0 901687 18 9

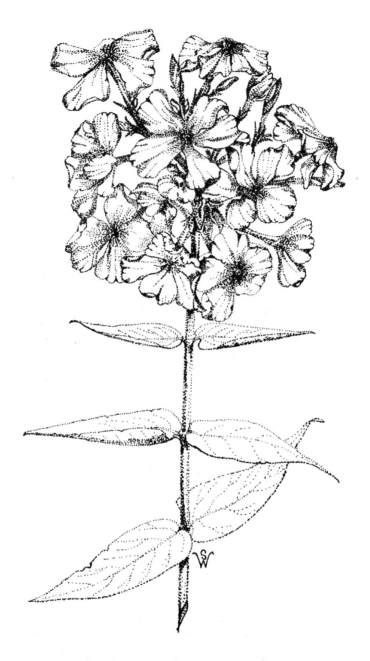

Phlox paniculata '**Chintz**' (*see page 22*)

Phlox in the Garden

The genus *Phlox* contains a wealth of plants that are invaluable in the garden. They can be divided into three reasonably well-defined groups. The first group to come to mind when considering plants for the mixed or herbaceous border is *Phlox paniculata* with all its wonderful cultivars, and a few allied species, which are undoubtedly the most popular group for the hardy plant enthusiast. A second group is woodland species that are ideal for the front of any shady borders, in woodland, or in a shady part of a rock garden. The third group is small sun-loving species that are usually grown in the rock garden or alpine house, or as wall plants. Many of these are sufficiently robust to be used as an edging for a mixed border. A few of this last group need specialized treatment in an alpine house or raised scree bed and are not included in this booklet.

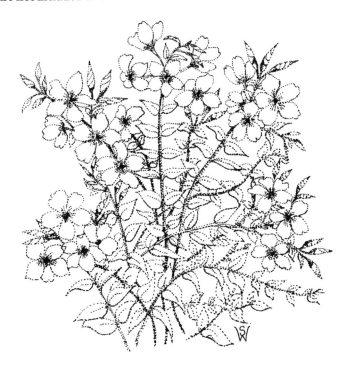

Phlox divaricata subsp. *laphamii* **'Chattahoochee'** (*see page 39*)

The Border Phlox

...the Phloxes in the garden-beds
Turn red, turn grey
With the time of day,
And smell sweet in the dusk, they die away
(Fredegond Shove, The Water-Mill)

*P*HLOX PANICULATA HAS BEEN GROWN and hybridised in British gardens for well over 250 years although recently its popularity appears to have fallen and very few nurseries now carry large selections of border phlox. However, despite its lack of availability through the trade, most gardens seem to have one or two, although few of them are named varieties. Fortunately there is now renewed interest in these plants and they are making a comeback.

The showy border phlox are increasingly being recognised as valuable additions to the summer garden. They normally start flowering in early July and continue until September or later, which helps fill the difficult month of August with colour and perfume. They are highly scented and have a similar colour range to the sweet peas, starting with icy white through pink and red to the darkest purple. They are clump forming and vary in height from 60-120cm (2-4ft). They can be grown in mixed borders or on their own. The white ones are quite difficult to place in the mixed colour beds but are lovely with blue, yellow or even purple. Other plants they associate particularly well with are monarda, aconitum and eupatorium. They are also excellent cut flowers for the house.

History

PHLOX PANICULATA IS A NATIVE of the eastern states in the USA. Overall there are some 67 species of phlox listed as growing in North America and they are all members of the *Polemoniaceae* (the polemonium family). The common name for *Phlox paniculata* in the States is the 'fall phlox'. It is a perennial with smooth-edged leaves arranged oppositely along the stem with flowers in terminal panicles. The flowers are lilac and stand at approximately 75-200cm (2½ -3½ ft.) high.

The first recorded cultivation of *Phlox paniculata* in this country was by Dr James Sherard (1666-1738) who was growing it in his botanical garden at Eltham, which was reputed to be the best-stocked in Europe. He commissioned Johan Jakob Dillenius to write and illustrate *Hortus Elthamensis*, an exotic catalogue of the plants he was growing. Published in 1732, this book included a drawing of *Phlox paniculata*, which at that time was labelled *Lychnidea folio salicino*. John Bartram, an American Quaker plant collector, sent *Lychnidea folio salicino* to Peter Collinson. He also sent *Phlox divaricata*, *Phlox subulata* and *Phlox maculata*. Peter Collinson, also a Quaker, was a great influence on the importation of plants from America. They corresponded and exchanged plants over many years and as late as 1765 he wrote to Bartram saying that it was wonderful to see the fertility of his country in phlox. Linnaeus considered Bartram to be the greatest natural botanist in the world.

Although, according to Loudon, the white form was not introduced until 1813, by 1829 he writes of phlox as a handsome plant in lively colours of red, white and purple. The first improved garden cultivar was attributed to George Wheeler, a nurseryman in Warminster in 1824. The main early hybridisers were the French. Lierval started in 1839 and various new forms rapidly appeared. By the 1880s they had introduced many cultivars but breeding was also being undertaken in England. James Douglas, writing in 1880, says in his book *Hardy Florists' Flowers*, "A friend who travelled in France last year and grows all the new phloxes, informs me that he did not see anything better than our own home-grown flowers". Downie & Laird in the north, and John Laing & Co. of Stanstead Park, Forest Hill were two particular breeders he mentions. The aim of the florists was to produce on the spike, individual flowers that were perfectly circular, with broad, wedge-shaped petals, which filled the space within their radius, even to the extent of their overlapping each other.

Phlox paniculata 'Iris', which received an Award of Merit in 1894, seems to be one of the earliest cultivars to survive to the present day. However, it is impossible to say with any certainty that the cultivar available now under this name is the original plant but it does fit the description fairly closely. Gertrude Jekyll used phlox extensively and they were an essential part of the Edwardian herbaceous border. Forbes of Hawick listed well over 300 cultivators in 1907 including a number of variegated varieties. H.J. Jones was an English breeder who was working just after the First World War introducing plants such as *P.p.* 'A.E. Amos' and *P.p.* 'Mrs A. Jeans'. Ruys, in The Netherlands, produced many excellent phlox including *P.p.* 'Caroline van den Berg' in 1928. Karl Foerster opened his nursery near Potsdam, Germany in 1903 but it was not until the 1930s that his phlox made their entrance. Over the next 40 years he introduced many good cultivars that are still with us today. He was very much a man after my own heart as he is famously quoted as saying, "A garden without phlox is not only a sheer mistake but a sin against the summer!" After the Second World War the really serious breeding of the modern phlox began with two Englishmen – Fred Simpson of Otley and Capt. B.H.B. Symons-Jeune, of Runnymede House, Old Windsor, who was famous for the rock gardens he created at Chelsea in the 1930s. Simpson produced two strains – the first with the prefix 'Otley' and then his Regal strain, all cultivars being named after royal palaces. A number of these are still available. Bakers of Codsall distributed Capt. Symons-Jeune's plants. They introduced around ten new cultivars a year from 1947 to the early 1960s although Capt. Symons-Jeune died at his home in Montego Bay, Jamaica on the 7th January, 1959.

They were followed by Alan Bloom who introduced a number of cultivars in the 1960s, two of which, *P.p.* 'Mother of Pearl' and *P.p.* 'Franz Schubert', are still very popular. Then came the new Dutch and German nurseries. In 1971 the zur Lindens introduced *P.p.* 'Flamingo', whose unique colour combination of salmon with purple eye has not been surpassed. I obtained their *P.p.* Blaue Gesine, introduced from Germany in 1993; it is an excellent blue and will, I hope, be taken up by a UK nursery. Piet Oudolf has also introduced some good plants: *P.p.* 'Blue Paradise' is always one of the first to flower and is a must for the border. In recent years the baton has been taken up by other Dutch growers who, by breeding short plants for the front of the border, are usefully extending the range. Very few old dwarf varieties have survived, *P.p.* 'Branklyn' being the only Victorian cultivar in commerce today. *P.p.* Mia Ruys from the 1920s is still around although it is difficult to buy the true cuiltivar; *P.p.* 'Little Boy', *P.p.* Eden's Flash and others have now arrived. These short plants are also being recommended for pot culture.

This is the way the Victorians used them although they did not confine themselves to short varieties. They grew them to give early season colour in the conservatory and then recommended that they should be planted out to give good plants in the garden the following year.

Phlox are also being developed for the cut flower trade. *P.p.* 'David' was, I understand, bred for this purpose and is a lovely garden plant. The latest trend is for mutant flowers with very reduced petals as in the René van Gaalen 'Feelings' series. So far he has introduced *P.p.* 'Empty Feelings', *P.p* 'Natural Feelings' and *P.p* 'Red Feelings', with *P.p* 'Strange Feelings' and others still to come. As the plants are sterile the flower heads are long-lived and thus good for the floristry trade.

Variegated *Phlox paniculata*

The first reference I have found for a variegated phlox is in Page's *Prodromus* published in 1818. He lists *Phlox suaveolens fol. varieg.* In the 1882 edition of Johnson's *Gardeners' Dictionary* it states that this plant was introduced in 1766. *Phlox suaveolens* is not now listed but Wherry, in his book *The Genus Phlox*, writes that *suaveolens* was an epithet applied to a form of *Phlox maculata* but there was not sufficient data to decide which subspecies they represented. This is most interesting because, if the plant was *maculata*, I am not aware of a variegated form in commerce today. However, by the early twentieth century there were a number of variegated *paniculata* varieties in cultivation. In Forbes of Hawick's catalogue of 1907 they listed four but by the 1920s these had disappeared.

The next cultivar to gain prominence was *P.p.* 'Norah Leigh' in the 1960s shortly followed by *P.p.* 'Harlequin'. 'Norah Leigh' was named after Mrs Joan Elliott's mother (the Elliotts being well-known nurserymen); the plant was found in her garden and Alan Bloom bulked it up for sale. Some years later when he was in the Munich Botanic garden he saw the same plant called *Phlox paniculata* 'Variegated'. It had been in the garden for some eighty years, which takes us back to the beginning of this century when Forbes were selling their French-bred plants. In recent years there has been a renewed interest in breeding phlox and *P.p.* 'Darwin's Joyce' has arrived on the scene. I find this a robust grower but it has now been decided that it is the same plant as *P.p.* 'Norah Leigh'. The number of variegated *Phlox paniculata* is growing rapidly, with new cultivars being introduced each year.

Identification

THE NAMING OF THE BORDER PHLOX is in a terrible muddle. For some reason, maybe the ease of propagation and the fact that they do not display well in containers in garden centres, phlox seem to pass from garden to garden and very quickly lose their names. They are incredibly difficult to identify definitively because they change colour throughout the day, according to light and temperature. They also change colour as they age. Leaf colour and form vary slightly; height, although usually a good guide can be affected by growing conditions.

The colour of the emerging shoots in spring does vary quite considerably but quickly becomes a fairly uniform green. The dark purple and red flowered varieties usually produce very dark and bronzed shoots whereas those with white flowers have lighter green leaves but this is not always the case. *P.p.* 'Hampton Court' (heliotrope) and *P.p.* 'Starfire' (crimson) retain the dark foliage all season.

The 'blue' phlox change colour according to the time of day and weather conditions. In the early morning, in the evening and on very dark, wet days they are the most beautiful luminous shades of blue but at mid-day during hot sunshine they turn a very bright mauve/puce colour. The species *Phlox paniculata* also displays this trait although it is not quite so pronounced as with some of the cultivars.

The colour of the buds is often a helpful guide when trying to identify a certain plant. The shape of the individual flower pips, or florets, on a panicle is also very useful. There are a number of pip shapes. The original *Phlox paniculata* (see illustration, p.26) has a small star shaped pip but with breeding the shape has been altered. Breeders have been seeking to produce large, flat round pips (see illustration of *P.p.* 'Grey Lady', p.13) but there are many variations. Some are just large versions of the original star shape (see illustration of *P.p.* 'Chintz', p.2), some have pointed petals which look rather like a hydrangea flower, whilst others incurve very slightly to show the reverse of the petal. The panicles themselves vary from tight conical to large lax ones. The perfect triangular head, shaped like lilac, was much sought after by Capt. Symons-Jeune.

One of the main aids to identification is time of flowering. All phlox of one cultivar start flowering at exactly the same time whether pot or garden grown. The blue and light crimson ones such as *P.p.* 'Cool of the Evening' and *P.p.* 'Tenor' are usually the first, followed by the pinks and purples and finally the whites although, as always, there are exceptions. Those under the name 'White Admiral' are early to mid-season varieties but *P.p.* 'Mount Fuji' is always the last to flower. If you have two plants called say, 'Tenor', one of which flowers in July and the other in September although the colour may be the same they are most unlikely to be the same cultivar.

The border phlox is a plant that has continually been improved upon and new cultivars are still being produced, therefore over the years many almost identical flower colours have been introduced. Even with the aid of a colour chart it is almost impossible to distinguish the differences. There are lots of excellent phlox in gardens but I think it will be unlikely that we will be able to put a name to many of them. Nonetheless, they should still be cultivated and passed round gardens. There may be a case for using the term Group when identifying old cultivars such as, say the Rijnstroom Group to identify a group of almost identical coloured plants with no names.

There are also some very good plants with very small individual flowers that are Victorian in origin (see illustration, p.13). They are often found growing in old and cottage gardens, where they have been for many generations. Until very recently I could say with certainty that these small flowered plants were all Victorian. However, with the introduction, in the 1990s, of the modern cultivars with small flowers confusion may arise in the future but if a plant has been in a garden for more than 15 years it is almost certain to be a very old cultivar.

Cultivation

PHLOX ARE HAPPY IN OPEN BORDERS IN SUN or very light shade and the soil needs to be moisture retentive but not waterlogged. *Phlox paniculata* itself and cultivars close to the original species such as *P.p.* 'Alba Grandiflora' seem to grow very happily on the lighter chalk soils for many years without disturbance but most of the other cultivars do require a deeper, heavier soil and regular division. If phlox are grown in deep shade they are much more difficult to establish and do not always flower so well.

Phlox should be fed in spring with an organic fertiliser such as dried pelleted chicken manure. If they are grown in a mixed border make sure that other neighbours do not swamp the emerging shoots. If they get over-shadowed by larger plants they will not flourish and very often do not flower at all. Established plants can be restricted to say 4 to 6 heads, the smaller the number of flower heads the larger the size of the panicles. I don't restrict my plants but I do cut the front stems down to about 22cm (9in); this prolongs the flowering period and helps to keep the plant looking tidy. If the back stems are cut down when they have flowered those in front will grow up to cover to them. The timing of the cutback depends rather on the season but I have a friend who gives her tall herbaceous plants what she calls the 'Chelsea Chop' in late May and this seems to be around the best time. Phlox do not normally require staking; they should have lower growing plants surrounding their feet as no matter how well grown the plants are, the bottom 22cm (9in) or so always tends to look rather tatty. Plants should be deadheaded to encourage re-flowering and to prevent self-sown seeds getting into a group of plants, thus losing the original named cultivar. Deadheading also helps prolong the season.

Phlox roots are fibrous and shallow and therefore need a good mulch in autumn; this also helps to retain moisture the following summer. They are gross feeders and plants should be split every three years although a very slow growing cultivar can be left for four years. I now prefer to split plants every three years irrespective of whether they look as though they need dividing; if left longer I find that although the plant seems healthy, it suddenly starts to die back in the centre and quite often does not re-appear the following spring. When a plant is weak it becomes susceptible to disease and it is far better to have two or three smaller plants making up a clump rather than one very large plant. If, due to lack of space, it is necessary to replant in the same place fresh compost should always be placed around the roots. Plants left growing on the same site without replenishment deteriorate and become susceptible to disease.

When moving phlox to a different part of the garden try to remove all the roots, otherwise it may be found that the original plant is difficult to eradicate. *P.p.* 'Mount Fuji' and *P.p.* 'Franz Schubert' are very vigorous and when moved tend to leave a trail of plants behind. Another plant that often causes confusion is *P.p.* 'Norah Leigh'. If this cultivar is moved, any plants coming from roots left in the ground lose their variegation but the white flowers with a lilac eye are very pretty against the plain green leaves.

Phlox are not easy to grow well in containers and plants purchased later in the season may well have lost leaves and look rather sorry for themselves. However, as long as a plant is basically healthy it can be cut down, re-potted and fed with a liquid fertiliser and the plant should grow away well. It can then either be planted in the garden or over-wintered in a cold frame or greenhouse and planted out in the spring. I garden on cold heavy clay and never plant any herbaceous plants in the autumn.

Propagation

PHLOX PANICULATA CAN BE PROPAGATED in a number of ways:

Root cuttings taken from September to spring are the safest way to ensure healthy plants and a large number of plants can be raised in this way. However, it does take at least two years to achieve a good flowering plant. To take root cuttings: dig up the plant and shake the soil from the roots. Cut the strongest roots into approximately 5cm (2in) lengths, and ensure that there is at least one bud. If you gently run your fingers along the root, you should feel a small bud, which is the 'eye' that forms the new plant. Lay the cuttings lengthways on the potting compost, in either trays or wide flowerpots and cover with a grit/potting compost mixture or vermiculite. Alternatively, plant a single root vertically in a small pot. To ensure that the root is inserted into the pot the correct way up, it is always useful to differentiate between the top and the bottom by making a sloping cut for the bottom and a straight one for the top.

Water and cover the pot with polythene then place in garden frame or cold greenhouse. A little bottom heat can speed up the process but is not essential.

'Irishman's cuttings' and soft tip cuttings taken from February through to mid-summer are a quick and easy method but be sure that the parent plant is absolutely free from disease; if there is the slightest doubt about this only root cuttings should be used. 'Irishman's cuttings' are taken early in the season and are small shoots which, when removed from the parent plant, already have roots; they just require to be potted up. Phlox root and grow quickly, so plants must be regularly potted-on to ensure large, healthy plants.

To make a tip cutting remove a non-flowering shoot 5-8cm (2-3in) long just below a leaf. Trim away the lower leaves and insert the cutting in gritty compost. Water and cover for about two weeks. Hormone rooting powder can be used but I have found that the cuttings root very easily without it. If these cuttings are taken late in the season, they must be showing a bud at the base of the stem before autumn or it is unlikely that they will survive the winter.

Splitting established clumps in small sections is also very easy; again the plant must be healthy. This can be done either in September after flowering or in the spring, depending upon the soil conditions. If plants are split regularly they can very easily be cut with a large carving knife or small saw but if the plant has been left too long and the centre is woody the old fashioned method of two forks back-to-back is the best way. The young outside parts of the plant should be re-planted and the old woody centre discarded. Do not be tempted to try and revive the centre - thriving new shoots will not be formed and a weak plant is liable to attract diseases.

Whilst named cultivars can only be reproduced vegetatively, phlox can, of course, also be grown from seed. Continental breeders are trying to breed mildew-resistant plants and are going for smaller individual pips.

1. *Phlox paniculata*
2. *P.p.* 'Victorian Lilac'
3. *P.p.* 'Alba Grandiflora'
4. *P.p.* 'San Antonio'
5. *P.p.* 'Grey Lady'
6. *P.p.* 'David'
7. *P.p.* 'Cool of the Evening'
8. *P.p.* 'Prospero'
9. *P.p.* 'Chintz'

Phlox paniculata and cultivars: detail of pip shapes

Pests and Diseases

A GREAT DEAL HAS BEEN WRITTEN in recent years about the new phlox, which have been bred to be mildew-resistant. Mildew may be a major problem in the USA but here in the UK plants, if well grown, do not normally suffer mildew until after flowering and only then in exceptionally hot, dry summers when the blue and purple cultivars are usually the first to become infected. Giving a couple of preventative sprays in June and July, when spraying the roses and hellebores, is usually sufficient; it is also beneficial to ensure that air can circulate through the plants. A good mulch helps preserve water but if it becomes necessary to water artificially the hose should be directed to the roots in order to avoid wetting the leaves. Artificial watering seems to encourage mildew but in a naturally wet season, such as the summer of 2000, plants were very happy. If the season has an early cool wet spell followed by a hot dry one, splitting of the stems can occur, which weakens them and makes them rather brittle but provided they are not broken off they will flower quite happily.

Eelworm was the scourge of phlox in the past but nurseries are now selling clean stock and the old plants that are still growing very well in the gardens appear to be resistant. Paul Nypes first described the disease in 1898. Eelworm (*Ditylenchus dispsaci*) is a stem-borne nematode, which is almost colourless, very thin and about 1-2mm long. It is virtually invisible to the naked eye, but if a small piece of infected stem and leaf are cut up and left in a glass of clean water for about half an hour the eelworms can be seen with a magnifying glass. In late autumn the eelworm passes from the diseased stems into the surrounding soil, then, as soon as growth re-starts, they make their way up the stems of host plants. The disease is identified by split stems (although this can also be caused by poor culture, see above), very narrow, distorted and twisted leaves, stems which are elongated and soft or stunted and swollen. The diseased stems produce very poor flowers or none at all. As yet there is no effective pesticide available to the amateur grower so if eelworm is present the plant must be destroyed and the ground not used for phlox again for at least three years. To prevent the eelworms hibernating over the winter the stems should be cut as low possible in the autumn. Debris from phlox should not be used for compost. If the plant is very precious, root cuttings can be taken, as eelworm is present only in the stem, not in the root. If root cuttings are made from diseased plants all soil must be washed from the root before the cutting is taken. Variegated plants cannot, of course, be propagated from root cuttings.

Virus can also cause wilt and either a stem or whole plant just withers and dies but the same effect can be caused by lack of water, particularly in the large dense clumps with woody centres.

Greenfly and other aphids, particularly on pot grown plants, can also cause distorted leaves and they must be sprayed at the first signs in order to prevent diseases being spread.

Although generally, slugs and snails do not seem to be particularly partial to phlox they do attack some of the slow growing, pale pink cultivars such as *P.p.* 'Rapture', *P.p.* 'Rosa Pastell' and *P.p.* 'Duchess of York'.

An eelworm-infected phlox

15

THE FOLLOWING LIST OF CULTIVARS is arranged alphabetically within colour bands; because many of the cultivars are of such similar colour I believe this will make identification easier. As explained above (p. 8) all those given in the blue/lilac range change colour with the time of day. *Phlox paniculata* plant hunting can be quite a time-consuming pastime as very few nurseries hold a wide range but most of those listed can be found. Many of the new Dutch cultivars are becoming quite widely available through the wholesale trade but it is the old varieties, which have stood the test of time as good garden plants, that need to be tracked down through the small specialist nurseries who still propagate their own plants. As an aid to identification I have also included a number, with their original descriptions, which have either recently disappeared from *The RHS Plant Finder* or are not currently commercially available but which it is to be hoped will be re-introduced over the next few seasons. All border phlox have a wonderful fragrance that is so evocative of summer. For this reason fragrance is not mentioned for every plant; the whites may have a slightly stronger perfume than the coloured phlox but the scent from a vase of mixed cultivars can be almost overpowering.

The border phlox can vary in height according to the soil conditions and the season. In a wet cold season the plants can be as much as 15cm (6in) taller than in a hot dry one. I have, therefore, indicated a range rather than an exact height in average growing conditions: "short" - under 90cm (3ft); "medium" - between 90 and 120cm (3-4ft); and "tall" - over 1.2m (4ft). It should be noted that many of the modern short cultivars, which have been raised with container growing in mind, are taller when well grown in the open garden.

Zone 4

WHITE

Phlox paniculata var. *alba*
The true white version of *P. paniculata* does not seem to be available commercially in the U.K. (see *P.p.* 'Alba Grandiflora' below) but the plant that is available in the Netherlands fits the original 1838 description by George Don of "being more robust than the typical species and white with a tinge of red." This is an excellent form that should be more widely used in this country. Mid-season. Tall.

P.p. 'Alba Grandiflora' AGM
An excellent white that is very often sold as *P.p.* var. *alba*. This plant is very drought tolerant and is much happier on shallow chalk soil than

some of the large flowered hybrids. The flowers are very like the species. Mid-season. Tall.

***P.p.* 'David'** (*Dr Hans Simon in Germany. Richard Simon of Brandywine River Museum, Pennsylvania, U.S.A. introduced in the States.1991*)
A spontaneous seedling. Flowers clear white. Light green foliage. Late-season. Medium.

***P.p.* 'Eden's Glory'** (*Introduced by Jacob Th. De Vroomen, Russell IL, 60075, Netherlands. 2000*)
Pure white flowers with light green foliage. Mid-season. Short.

***P.p.* 'Kelways Cherub'** (*Kelways, England. c1930*)
Ivory white. The plant currently available in commerce is so close to *P.p.* 'Mount Fuji' as to be almost indistinguishable. Late season. Tall.

***P.p.* 'Mia Ruys'** (*B. Ruys, Kwekerij Moerheim, Dedemsvaart, Netherlands. 1922*)
Pure white. Short.

***P.p.* 'Miranda'** (*Introduced in 1998 by Blackmore & Langdon, Pensford, Nr Bristol BS39 4JL*)
'Miranda' (Prospero's daughter) is a sport from 'Prospero'. It is almost white but with a very slight blush of lavender. Early. Medium.

***P.p.* 'Miss Universe'** (*Ad. & Mart Vester B.V. 1996. Reg. No. 90*)
Pure white. Hybrid from the cultivars 'Rembrandt' and 'Bright Eyes'. Medium.

***P.p.* 'Mount Fuji'** AGM (syns. 'Mount Fujiyama' & 'Fujiyama') (U.S.A. c1970)
Pure white. Flowers borne in dense long, conical heads on very sturdy stems. Upright, clump forming. Usually the last phlox to flower. Tall.

***P.p.* 'Nymphenburg'** (*Buchner, Germany, 1954*)
White. Very tall. Early

***P.p.* 'Pax'** (*A. Schöllhammer, Langenargen am Bodensee, Germany. 1950*)
White with yellow stamens. Medium.

***P.p.* 'Rembrandt'** (*B. Ruys, Kwekerij Moerheim, Dedemsvaart, Netherlands*)
Creamy white with very slight green throat. Well-formed classic triangular heads with medium sized pips. Good light green foliage. Mid-season. Short.

***P.p.* 'Schneerausch'** (Snowdrift) (*K. Foerster, Bornim, Germany. 1947*)
Large distinctive ice white flowers with a purple tinge to the buds. Mid-season. Medium.

***P.p.* 'Snow White'**
Pure white flowers with small green throat. Pale green leaves. Short.

***P.p.* 'White Admiral'** AGM (*c1955*)
White with eye of greenish cream. There are as many versions of 'White Admiral' as of the "ubiquitous pink". Every county has its own 'White Admiral'. Vigorous growth. Early. Medium.

WHITE WITH PINK EYE

***P.p.* 'Blue Ice'** AGM (*c1988*)
Pink buds open to reveal startling white flowers with a deeper pink eye. At times these appear to have a bluish tinge. Short.

***P.p.* 'Europa'** (syn. 'Europe') (*Pfitzer, Stuttgart, Germany. 1910*)
Snow white, carmine eye. This plant does not weather well – it goes very streaky with rain. Short.

***P.p.* 'Fidelio'** (*B. Ruys, Kwekerij Moerheim, Dedemsvaart, Netherlands.* 1939)
Lovely tall white, with large neat cerise eye. One of the best with this colour combination. Medium.

***P.p.* 'Graf Zeppelin'** (Count Zeppelin) (*W. Pfitzer, Stuttgart, Germany. c1939*)
Chalk white, red eye. Medium.

***P.p.* 'Kirmeslaendler'** (*K. Foerster, Bornim, Germany. 1935*)
White with distinct red eye. Does have a tendency to streak. Vigorous and late flowering. Very tall.

***P.p.* 'Miss Holland'** (*Ad. & Mart Vester B.V. 1996. Reg No 89*)
White with eye red. Hybrid from the cultivars 'Rembrandt' and 'Bright Eyes'. Late flowering. Medium.

***P.p.* 'Pat Coleman'**
White with a lilac eye. Very similar to a reverted 'Norah Leigh'. Mid-season. Medium.

***P.p.* 'Popeye'** (*René van Gaalen, Den Hoom, Netherlands. 1992*)
White flushed with a very pale peach/pink with a darker eye. Strong stems. Early. Medium.

***P.p.* 'Prime Minister'** (*Earliest reference found 1961 in Canadian catalogue*)
Pure white with a violet eye. Medium.

WHITE/LILAC

***P.p.* 'Franz Schubert'** (*A. Bloom, Bressingham, Norfolk, England. 1980*)
Named in honour of Alan Bloom's favorite composer. Its colour is near to Parma violet, with just a tinge of pink. A very vigorous grower. Mid-season. Tall.

***P.p.* 'Grey Lady'** (*post-World War 2*)
Blue-grey, white centre. Shoots bright green in spring. Early. Medium.

***P.p.* 'Iceberg'** *(B.H.B. Symons -Jeune. 1949)*
White, shaded violet, with slightly deeper coloured buds and throat. Mid-season. Medium.

***P.p.* 'Lavendelwolke'** (Lavender Cloud) *(K. Foerster, Bornim, German. 1939)*
Very pale lilac, almost white. Late. Medium.

***P.p.* 'Miss Kelly'**
Parma violet, with just a tinge of pink. Very similar to 'Franz Schubert', slight bluer, possibly shorter. Early. Tall.

***P.p.* 'Prospero'** AGM *(K. Foerster, Bornim, Germany. 1956)*
White flushed with purple/violet, except at margins, and cream eye; colour fading slightly with maturity. This is an excellent plant. Shoots mid to dark green in spring, leaves narrower than average rather like *P.p.* 'Alba Grandiflora'. There is an unresolved muddle over the naming of this plant, as *P.p.* 'Sternhimmel' as grown in Holland and Germany is identical to the 'Prospero' grown in England. Early. Tall.

***P.p.* 'Sternhimmel'** *(A. Schölhammer, Langenargen am Bodensee, Germany. 1942)*
White and lilac. Identical to 'Prospero'. Early. Tall.

***P.p.* 'Violetta Gloriosa'** *(K. Foerster, Bornim, Germany. 1956)*
Pale lilac fading to almost white and then darkening with age. Again, very similar to 'Prospero'. Early. Medium.

PALE PINK

***P.p.* 'Dresden China'** *(B.H.B. Symons-Jeune. 1947 - In first batch of 12 he introduced)*
An exquisite soft shell-pink streaked lake deepening at eye with age. Free flowering and very luminous. Mid-season. Tall.

***P.p.* 'Elizabeth Arden'** *(B.H.B. Symons-Jeune. Pre1956)*
A lovely soft pink with deeper eye. Medium.

***P.p.* 'Fairy's Petticoat'** *(B.H.B. Symons-Jeune. Pre1956)*
A really lovely variety in a delicate shade of soft mulberry on light ground with slightly deeper eye. Sturdy and vigorous, the heads are compact but somewhat elongated with immense pips of perfect shape. Mid-season. Tall.

***P.p.* 'Lady Clare'** Large, pale pink flowers - possibly a seedling by B.H.B. Symons-Jeune and named by a nurseryman. Late. Medium.

***P.p.* 'Mirabelle'** *(Introduced in 1998 by Blackmore & Langdon, Pensford, Nr Bristol)*
A very delicate, pale pink with a slightly deeper eye. Mid-season. Medium.

***P.p.* 'Monica Lynden-Bell'** *(Monica Lynden-Bell c1970s)*
Soft pale shell-pink. Seedling found in Hampshire by Monica Lynden-

Bell, who won many prizes at local flower shows with it. Mid-season. Medium.

***P.p.* 'Mother of Pearl'** AGM (*A. Bloom, Bressingham, Norfolk, England. 1954*)

White, suffused pink. A very distinctive cultivar with slightly cupped flowers. Medium.

***P.p.* 'Mrs A. Jeans'** (*H.J. Jones, England. Prior to 1922*)

Delicate pink/mauve on a white ground with white eye. Mid-season. Medium.

***P.p.* 'P.D. Williams'** (*B. Ruys, Kwekerij Moerheim, Dedemsvaart, Netherlands. 1932*)

Apple-blossom pink, darker centre. Named after P.D. Williams who owned the famous garden of Lanarth, near St Keverne in the west of Cornwall. One of his greatest gardening friends was Capt. William Pinwall of Trehane. Medium.

***P.p.* 'Rapture'** (*B.H.B. Symons-Jeune. England. 1958*)

Delicate shade of rose-pink, with a fuchsia-pink centre radiating a slight sheen over the whole flower. The pips are of good size and heads exceptionally large for a low growing variety. Mid-July. This is not a vigorous grower but it is well worth persevering with. Short.

***P.p.* 'Rosa Pastell'** (*K. Foerster, Bornim, Germany. 1947*)

An excellent pale pink that is a mid season variety with a very long flowering period. Medium.

***P.p.* 'Rosa Spier'** (*B. Ruys, Kwekerij Moerheim, Dedemsvaart, Netherlands. 1953*)

Large pale pink flowers with a slightly darker eye. Medium.

PINK

***P.p.* 'Balmoral'** (*Fred M. Simpson, Otley, Yorkshire, England*)

Extra large heads of clear light rose pink, strong grower. Medium.

***P.p.* 'Bill Green'** (*A. Bloom, Bressingham, Norfolk, England. 1978*)

Deep pink with a conspicuous crimson eye. Neat tidy habit. Named in memory of a long-standing nursery foreman, at Blooms of Bressingham, who died prematurely. Short.

***P.p.* 'B. Symons-Jeune'** (*B.H.B. Symons-Jeune, England. 1947 - In first batch of 12 introduced*)

The colour is rose-pink with a large and distinct carmine crimson eye, giving a delightful effect. Strong and vigorous in habit. Named after Capt. Symons-Jeune who, in the late 1940s and early 50s, bred a greatly improved strain of *Phlox paniculata*. The flowers were very large and colours ranged from pale blue to rich purple. Short.

P.p. **'Bright Eyes'** AGM (*B.H.B. Symons-Jeune, England. 1967*)
The original catalogue description was "An enchanting new phlox with a real 'twinkle'. Flower pips of a pleasing pale pink with a fine crimson eye to provide that happy contrast." Medium.

P.p. **'Cinderella'** (*B.H.B. Symons-Jeune, England 1949*)
A pale mulberry-pink with bright carmine eye. Good truss, ideal for front of border. Short.

P.p. **'Chintz'** (*B.H.B. Symons-Jeune, England 1956*)
A strong growing phlox, distinct from most of the Symons-Jeune types in that the individual pips are large versions of the species shape. The colouring is pink with full centre of bright crimson, the truss compact with enormous pips. Late. Tall.

P.p. **'Discovery'**
Warm soft pink. Short.

P.p. **'Dodo Hanbury-Forbes'** AGM (syn. 'Dorothy Hanbury-Forbes') (*B.H.B. Symons-Jeune, England. 1956*)
Produces a triangular truss of magnificent clear pink. Named after the wife of Cecil Hanbury and the sister of Capt Symons-Jeune. She and her brother planned many new developments at her home, La Mortola, in Italy. After her husband's death she married a former chaplain to the Speaker of the House of Commons. She restored the gardens at La Mortola after the 1939-45 war. Mid-season. Medium.

P.p. **'Eden's Crush'** (*Introduced by Jacob Th. de Vroomen, Russell IL, 60075, Netherlands. 2000*)
Vibrant dark pink with a darker eye. Short.

P.p. **'Eden's Flash'** (*Introduced by Jacob Th. de Vroomen, Russell IL, 60075, Netherlands. 2000*)
Pink with slightly lighter edges. Suitable for growing in containers. Medium.

P.p. **'Eva Cullum'** (*A. Bloom, Bressingham, Norfolk, England. 1978*)
Warm pink with red eye. Strong, leafy habit. Named after the person who headed the retail department at Bressingham until her retirement in 1965. Medium.

P.p. **'Glamis'** (*Fred M. Simpson, Otley, Yorkshire, England*)
Fuchsia-pink with purple eye. The plants are exceptionally well furnished with side branches, all of which carry heavy trusses of bloom with pips of outstanding size and good formation. Medium.

P.p. **'Judy'** (*Gebr. Van de Reep, Hillegom, Netherlands. 1983*)
Rose pink. Short.

P.p. **'Lichtspel'** (*Piet Oudolf, Hummelo, Netherlands. 1990*)
Small lavender pink flowers with a deep pink eye. Tall.

***P.p.* 'Little Princess'**
Bright pink with a paler eye. Early. Short.

***P.p.* 'Lizzy'** (*H. Oudshoorn, Rijpwatering, Netherlands. 1999*)
Bright pink with white eye. Early. Short.

***P.p* 'Mies Copijn'** (*H. Copijn, Groenekan, Holland. c1951*)
Flesh pink with rose edge. Splendid habit of growth; strong perfect truss. Very distinct. Medium.

***P.p.* 'Miss Elie'**
Bright rose pink flowers. Mid-season. Tall.

***P.p.* 'Miss Pepper'** (*G. Bartels, Aalsmeer, Netherlands. 1992*)
Dark red shoots in spring give rise to small pink flowers with a red eye. An excellent modern introduction. Late flowering. Tall.

***P.p.* 'Mrs Milly van Hoboken'** (*B. Ruys, Kwekerij Moerheim, Dedemsvaart, Netherlands. 1922*)
Has enormous flowers of soft pink. One of the best. Medium.

***P.p.* Rainbow'**
The flowers are various shades of pink, with a paler eye. Early. Short.

***P.p.* 'Sandringham'** (*Fred M. Simpson, Otley, Yorkshire, England*)
Persian rose with slightly darker centre. The plants are exceptionally well furnished with side branches, all of which carry heavy trusses of bloom with pips of outstanding size and good formation. Spring shoots dark green/flushed purple, fading with age. Late. Medium.

***P.p.* 'Starburst'** (*Introduced by Jacob Th. de Vroomen, Russell IL, 60075, Netherlands. 2000*)
Small rosy-pink flowers with yellowish cream edges. This is an unusual colour combination that requires careful placing in the border. Early season. Tall.

UBIQUITOUS PINK

In almost every cottage garden there is a good, standard pink phlox. They are almost identical with perhaps the minutest difference, making it impossible to distinguish one from the other. The following are the original descriptions but the cultivars that are commercially available all seem the same "ubiquitous pink". They are, however, still very good phlox and have stood the test of time.

***P.p.* 'Coral Queen'**
Rose-pink flowers. This cultivar is extremely accommodating; it will tolerate more shade than most and has a very long flowering period. Mid-late season. Medium

P.p. **'Jules Sandeau'** (identical to 'Württembergia') AM 1922 (*V. Lemoine, Nancy, France. 1911*)
Rose pink. Very large flowers. The true 'Jules Sandeau' is dwarf. Short.

P.p. **'Otley Choice'** (*Fred M. Simpson, Otley, Yorkshire, England*)
Large pink flowers with deeper eye. Medium.

P.p. **'Pastorale'** (*K. Foerster, Bornim, Germany, Bornim. 1947*)
Large flowers salmon/pink with darker eye. Medium.

P.p. **'Rijnstroom'** (*F. Koppius, Kwekerij Rijnstroom, Alphen an der Rijn, Netherlands. c 1910*)
Fine pink. This is the plant that has to a very large extent become the true ubiquitous pink. Medium.

SALMON PINK

P.p. **'Annie Laurie'** (*Earliest reference: The RHS Journal, 1915, from Messrs. W. Wells, Merstham*)
Bright rich salmon, eye deep rose – has a tendency to burn. Medium.

P.p. **'Apple Blossom'** (*Earliest reference 'New' in Baker's 1925 catalogue*)
A beautiful and delicate shade of soft pink, shading to white in centre; paler edition of the popular 'Elizabeth Campbell'. Medium.

P.p. **'Duchess of York'** (*c1930*)
Soft salmon pink with a white eye. Late. Medium.

P.p. **'Elizabeth Campbell'** (*Earliest reference: The RHS Journal, 1910, exhibited by Messrs. W. Wells, Merstham*)
Light salmon changing to pink in centre. This is another old cultivar that, as far as I am aware, is not in commerce. Medium.

P.p. **'Endurance'** (*B. Symons-Jeune. Pre 1956*)
Deep salmon-orange with distinct and pleasing carmine eye. Given the name 'Endurance' because it remains in flower over a long period. Huge, well shaped pips on compact heads. Short.

P.p. **'Eva Foerster'** (syn. 'Salmon Beauty') (*K. Foerster, Bornim, Germany. 1934*)
Very large flowers, rich salmon-pink with white eye. Short.

P.p. **'Firefly'** (*Symons-Jeune. 1956*)
Clearest pink-peach with a bright crimson eye. Medium.

P.p. **'Flamingo'** (*zur Linden, Bissendorf-Linne, Germany. 1971*)
Bright salmon pink with neat crimson eye. This unique colour combination makes this a very distinctive plant. Mid-season. Medium.

P.p. **'Mary Fox'** (*A. Bloom, Bressingham, Norfolk, England. 1975*)
A fine head of bright salmon-pink unlike any other. Named after the lady who was in charge of the nursery office at Bressingham from 1951 until she

retired in 1984. Mid-season. Medium.

***P.p.* 'Mrs Fincham'** (*Earliest reference Blackmore & Langdon, 1957*)
Salmon-pink. Medium.

***P.p.* 'Sir John Falstaff'** (*Earliest reference Bakers of Codsall, Autumn 1949*)
A deep salmo- pink. Symons-Jeune said this appeared with a fanfare of
trumpets but to his mind, although the pips and the height were good,
the head was large and branching, so that it was not improved by a
shower of rain. He expressed doubt that his grandchildren would grow it.
Tall.

***P.p.* 'Steeple Bumpstead'** (*1990s Paul Durrant*)
Seedling from Paul Durrant, large heads of starry salmon-pink flowers
with a vivid purple eye. Medium.

***P.p.* 'Sweetheart'** (*Earliest reference AM August 15, 1928*)
Rich salmon-red with crimson eye. Short.

***P.p.* 'Visions'**
Warm salmon-pink flowers with a darker eye. Short.

***P.p.* 'Windsor'** AGM, AM 1957. (*Fred M. Simpson, Otley, Yorkshire, England*)
Brightest salmon pink. Medium.

LAVENDER/BLUE

P. paniculata
Small, star shaped soft lilac flowers. Mid-season. Tall.

***P.p.* 'Blaue Gesine'** (*zur Linden, Bissendorf-Linne, Germany. 1993*)
Lavender blue with a tinge of pink; well-shaped triangular head, medium
sized pips. Leaves retain a slight purple at tips and edges. Early. Tall.

***P.p.* 'Blue Boy'** (*B.H.B. Symons-Jeune, England. 1949*)
The original description said "This is the nearest to a blue phlox yet
produced; is of medium height and a good grower." Very few of the
plants offered commercially fit this description. Medium.

***P.p.* 'Blue Evening'** (*Piet Oudolf, Hummelo, Netherlands. 1990*)
Slatey lavender-blue, large *paniculata* shaped pips. The colour is almost
identical to 'Cool of the Evening' but because of the shape of the pips it
looks very different. Slightly taller than average. Early. Tall.

***P.p.* 'Blue Mist'** (*B.H.B. Symons- Jeune, England. 1949*)
Soft magenta with blue-grey blaze, the whole becoming blue-grey when
expanded. The pips are huge with a good truss on an unusually stocky plant.
Medium.

***P.p.* 'Blue Moon'** (*B.H.B. Symons- Jeune, England. 1949*)
Pastel lilac-blue with large, well shaped individual florets. Turns a
wonderful blue in the half-light. Robust. Medium.

P.p. **'Blue Paradise'** (*Piet Oudolf, Hummelo, Netherlands. 1990*)
Indigo. An excellent modern phlox that is probably the darkest of the blues. Spring shoots green, flushed purple, fading with age. The flower buds are also attractive with a dark purple tinge. Large panicles with hydrangea shaped pips. Early. Tall.

P.p. **'Bonny Maid'** (*B.H.B. Symons-Jeune, England. 1962*)
Light lavender-blue, flushed mauve. Very large heads. Spring shoots dark green/flushed purple, fading with age. Early. Medium.

P.p. **'Caroline van den Berg'** (*B. Ruys, Kwekerij Moerheim, Dedemsvaart, Netherlands. 1927*)
Attractive flowers of deep lavender-blue with petals that incurve slightly to show a silvery reverse. Spring shoots dark green/flushed purple, fading with age. Not particularly good foliage but should be grown nonetheless. Mid-season. Medium.

P.p. **'Cool of the Evening'** (*B.H.B. Symons-Jeune, England. Pre 1956*)
Slatey lavender-blue with slightly deeper centre. Well shaped. Spring shoots green tinged with purple. The flower buds are also attractive with a dark purple tinge. Truly magical in the cool of the evening. Early. Medium.

P.p. **'Eden's Smile'** (*Introduced by Jacob Th. de Vroomen, Russell IL, 60075, Netherlands. 2000*)
Mauve with very large flower heads, Mid-season. Short.

P.p. **'Etoile de Paris'** see 'Toits de Paris'

P.p. **'Eventide'** (*B.H.B. Symons-Jeune. 1947. In the first batch of 12 he introduced*)
A late flowering delicate lavender blue flushed lilac. It is for all practical purposes a self, but in the early stages there is an insignificant carmine marking at the centre. Medium.

P.p. **'Katrina'**
Lavender flowers. Late season. Medium

P.p. **'Lilac Time'** (*B.H.B. Symons-Jeune. Pre 1956*)
Symons-Jeune wrote that in his opinion this is the most beautiful phlox yet raised: "The 3ft 9in stems are strong and upstanding, and the 9in pyramid consists of well-shaped flowers. Individual pips are large, measuring 1¾in of the softest clear lilac tone that is cool and most restful, yet gleaming in the sunlight. It has a constitution which enables it to withstand the buffetings of our August gales." Tall.
'Lilac Time', is frequently incorrectly sold as 'Amethyst'.

P.p. **'Little Lovely'** (*B.H.B. Symons-Jeune. 1956*)
A charming semi-dwarf. Large, well shaped pips of a delightful shade of wood violet with a noticeable white eye. Short.

25

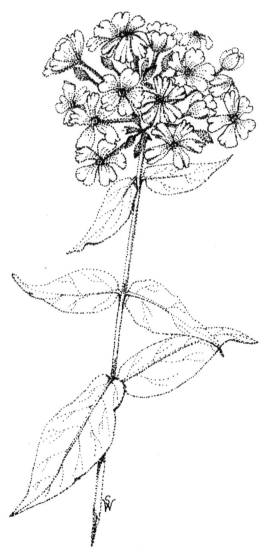

Phlox paniculata (*see page 24*)

P.p. **'Toits de Paris'** (syn. 'Etoile de Paris') (*B.H.B. Symons-Jeune, England. 1956*)

Lavender-blue with a sheen. The plant currently being sold as 'Toits de Paris' is in fact 'Cool of the Evening'. However, 'Etoile de Paris' is not a valid name and this plant is the true 'Toits de Paris'. Symons-Jeune's own description was "a soft lavender-blue which, seen in the evening light, turns a lovely pale blue so long wanted in a phlox. To many the name may seem unusual, but to those who have visited Paris it describes the colour of the roofs on a sunny evening after rain. The heads and pips are of medium size, but it is a free flowering sturdy variety and will be wanted on account of its enchanting colour". Early. Short.

SCARLET/CRIMSON

P.p. **'A. E. Amos'** (*H. J. Jones, England. 1920s*)

Soft-scarlet flowers in large, outstanding trusses. The very dark red shoots of spring pale with age. No real discernible difference between this and 'Tenor'. Medium.

P.p. **'Albert Leo Schlageter'** (syn. 'Leo Schlageter') (*L.G. Arends, Ronsdorf, Wuppertal, Germany. 1925*)

Brilliant scarlet-carmine, dark centre. Medium.

P.p. **'Eden's Glow'** (*Introduced by Jacob Th. de Vroomen, Russell IL, 60075, Netherlands. 2000*)

Vibrant orchid-pink flowers with light green foliage. Mid-season. Short.

P.p. **'Fesselballon'** (*K. Foerster, Bornim, Garmany, 1949*)

Bright rose-red with carmine eye. Medium. Mid-season.

P.p. **'Harewood'** (*Fred M. Simpson, Otley, Yorkshire, England*)

Bright rich carmine with magenta eye. Medium.

P.p. **'Inspiration'** (*B.H.B. Symons-Jeune, England. Pre1968*)

Attractive deep magenta or light crimson with slightly deeper eye. Provides a brave display in the garden, while the colour indoors is distinctive, particularly under artificial light. Medium.

P.p. **'Juliglut'** (July Glow) (*K. Foerster, Bornim, Germany. 1934*)

Very attractive glowing carmine-crimson. Very dark red shoots in spring. Foliage stays dark green. Always one of the first to flower in June, it flowers over a long period but is susceptible to mildew in hot, dry summers. Medium.

P.p. **'Kirchenfurst'** (*K. Foerster, Bornim, Germany. 1966*)

Very bright carmine red. Tall. Mid-season.

P.p. **'Look Again'** (*B.H.B. Symons-Jeune, England. 1968*)

Self-coloured rosy magenta flower. Medium.

***P.p.*'Otley Ideal'** (*Fred M. Simpson, Otley, Yorkshire, England*)
This was the first of a new generation of dwarf phlox from Fred Simpson.
Very compact growth, branching from ground level. One of the first to
flower with blooms of a brilliant cherry red with a dark eye. Short.

***P.p.* 'Red Riding Hood'** (*Introduced by Jacob Th. de Vroomen, Russell IL,
60075, Netherlands. 2001*)
The flowers are bright shiny red. Foliage is very dark green. Short.

***P.p.* 'Septemberglut'** (September Glow) (*L.G. Arends, Ronsdorf, Wuppertal,
Germany. 1918*)
Glowing salmon-scarlet with a cerise eye. Short.

***P.p.* 'Sir Malcolm Campbell'**
Intense crimson-carmine, strong habit. Medium.

***P.p.* 'Tenor'** (*K. Foerster, Bornim, Germany. 1939*)
A lovely soft scarlet/cerise - just a shade lighter than 'A. E. Amos'. Very
vigorous. In spring the emerging shoots are a very deep red but fade with
age to dark green foliage. In the south of England this is always one of the
first to flower in June. It flowers over a long period but is susceptible to
mildew. Medium.

PURPLE

***P.p.* 'Aida'** (*W. Pfitzer, Stuttgart, Germany. 1933*)
Crimson with purple eye that brings to mind the sumptuousness of
clerical vestments. Compact habit. Short.

***P.p.* 'Amethyst'** (*K. Foerster, Bornim, Germany. 1951*)
Deep lavender slightly suffused rose. *P.p.* 'Lilac Time' is often sold
incorrectly as 'Amethyst'. Medium.

***P.p.* 'Border Gem'** (*Fairburn, near Carlisle, England. 1913*)
Petunia purple with Tyrian purple eye. Spring shoots dark green/flushed
purple fading with age. Late. Short.

***P.p.* 'Branklyn'**
Attractive heads of deep lilac flowers with a white eye. Short stocky habit.
Grows stiffly with abundant foliage. This small flowered phlox is
Victorian and was re-named when recently reintroduced. Medium.

***P.p.* 'Croix de Malte'** (*Earliest reference R. C. Notcutt's catalogue, 1903*)
Large flowers with rosy violet Maltese Cross on a white background.
Mid-season. Short.

***P.p.* 'Duesterlohe'** (*K. Foerster, Bornim, Germany. 1962*)
Lovely rich, glowing purple and very luminous. Free flowering. Large
well shaped panicles slightly taller than average. Always one of the earliest
to flower. In very hot, dry periods the flower colour fades to a streaky

white but quickly reverts to normal when the weather conditions improve. Tall.

In commerce 'Duesterlohe' is sometimes sold incorrectly labelled as 'Nicky' and 'Eclaireur'.

***P.p.* 'Eclaireur'** (*V. Lemoine, Nancy, France. Pre-1892 - earliest reference G. Paul, 1892, when it was awarded an A.M.*)
Carmine violet red with pink centre. Purple leaves. As far as I am aware the true plant is not in commerce and plants sold under this name are likely to be 'Duesterlohe'. Medium.

***P.p.* 'Excelsior'** (*B.H.B. Symons-Jeune, England. 1958*)
Distinct shade of Dodge-purple flowers with a slightly deeper eye; well-formed heads and free flowering. Medium.

***P.p.* 'Hampton Court'** (*Fred M. Simpson, Otley, Yorkshire, England*)
Rich heliotrope blue with dark foliage. Good flower trusses, side branches well furnished with large sized pips. Late. Tall.

***P.p.* 'Iris'** (*Earliest ref: AM 1894*)
Lovely rich purple, with slight lightening at eye - beautiful and iridescent colour at night. Spring shoots dark green/flushed purple fading with age. Mid-season. Medium.

***P.p.* 'Laura'** (*PBR Flamingo International, Netherlands*)
Purple with white centre to the flowers. This plant is very similar to *P.p.* 'Uspekh'. Medium.

***P.p.* 'Le Mahdi'** AGM (*G. u. Koe. AM 15th August 1899*)
Bright royal purple, eye crimson. Mid-season. Short.

***P.p.* 'Little Boy'** Cerise flower with large white centre, round flowers, For front of border. Short.

***P.p.* 'Little Laura**
Purple flowers with white eye. Short.

***P.p.* 'Newbird'** (syn. 'Neubert') (*Germany. c1923*)
Rich amaranth crimson. Medium.

***P.p.* 'Nicky'** This is not a valid name and plants sold as 'Nicky' are identical to 'Duesterloe'. Tall.

***P.p.* 'Othello'** (*B.H.B. Symons-Jeune, England. 1960*)
A claret red, slightly deeper shade than 'Vintage Wine' with good-sized pips. While the heads are only of medium size, this is more than made good by the large quantity produced. Spring shoots dark green/flushed purple fading with age. Mid-season. Medium.

***P.p.* 'Otley Purple'** (*Fred M. Simpson, Otley, Yorkshire, England, 1956*)
Dianthus purple with a dark crimson eye. This plant is an excellent

early grower and flowers very early. The spring shoots are dark green/flushed purple, fading with age. Short.

***P.p.* 'Red Indian'** *(B.H.B. Symons-Jeune, England. Early 1950s)*
Vivid wine crimson with heads and pips of medium size, but of good form and quality. Late. Medium.

***P.p.* 'Russian Violet'** *(B.H.B. Symons-Jeune, England. Pre 1958)*
Rich violet purple, large well-formed heads and perfect pips; another triumph for the raiser, Capt. Symons-Jeune. Vigorous in habit. Medium.

***P.p.* 'San Antonio'** *(Büchner, Munchen, Germany. c1930)*
Crimson-lake magenta. The individual pips are large versions of the species shape. Early. Medium.

***P.p.* 'Skylight'** *(B.H.B. Symons-Jeune, England. 1956)*
Original description - "possibly the best of 'near blues' being close to the shade of Parma Violet. It not only shows up well in the border but also blends delightfully with richer colours. The stems are unusually strong, and the huge pips perfect in shape". The plant currently in circulation under this name is dark mauve/purple with white eye. Medium.

***P.p.* 'Starfire'** *(B. Ruys, Kwekerij Moerheim Dedemsvaart, Netherlands. 1937)*
Brightest crimson-red with dark-foliage. Holds its colour well. Vigorous habit. Mid-season. Medium.

***P.p.* 'The King'** *(U.S.A. c1939)*
Brightest purple-red. Late. Short. An earlier plant, also called 'The King', was pink but appears to have been lost prior to the introduction of the purple cultivar.

***P.p.* 'Uspekh'** *(P. G. Gaganov, Russia. 1937)*
Purple with a white starry centre. A phlox of Russian origins that has recently been introduced to the UK market. Vigorous. Medium.

***P.p.* 'Vintage Wine'** *(B.H.B. Symons-Jeune, England. 1957)*
Rich red claret. A phlox without reproach. Medium.

***P.p.* 'Wilhelm Kesselring'** *(B. Ruys, Kwekerij Moerheim, Dedemsvaart, Netherlands. 1923)*
Bright light reddish purple at eye, shades white. Short.

ORANGE/RED

***P.p.* 'Brigadier'** AGM *(Tho. Carlisle Ltd. Late 1940s)*
Salmon-scarlet near geranium lake. Early. Medium.

***P.p.* 'Cecil Hanbury'** *(B.H.B. Symons-Jeune, England.1947. In first batch of 12 he introduced)*
A glowing rich orange salmon enhanced with a small but vivid carmine eye. Named after Capt. Symons-Jeune's brother-in-law, who succeeded

his father Sir Thomas Hanbury in the ownership of the Botanical Gardens at La Mortola, Italy. Medium.

***P.p.* 'Charmaine'** (*B.H.B. Symons-Jeune, England. 1963*)
The original catalogue description said, "In this particular colour range, it will be very many years before this variety is superseded. It is really superb and blooms most profusely. The striking colour is best described as bright cherry-red with ivory blaze". The plant currently in commerce does not have a noticeable 'ivory blaze'. Medium

***P.p.* 'Frau Alfred von Mauthner'** (syn. 'Spitfire') (*B. Ruys, Kwekerij Moerheim, Dedemsvaart, Netherlands. 1927*)
Geranium lake with crimson eye. This plant has a sad history: it was named for a Hungarian lady who was a great amateur gardener. After the war many phlox of German origin were re-named and it was suggested that this plant should be called 'Spitfire'. Mr Ruys wrote to the RHS saying that the lady was of Jewish origin, and she had disappeared during the war. At that time there were no connections between Holland and Hungary so he thought that 'Spitfire' was a very good name and agreed to the re-naming. Medium.

***P.p.* 'Prince of Orange'** (syn. 'Orange Perfection') (*A. Schöllhammer, Langenargen am Bodensee, Germany. 1950*)
Orange-scarlet intense colour, not subject to scorching. Medium.

***P.p.* 'Spaetrot'** (syn 'Latest Red') (*K. Foerster, Bornim, Germany. 1930*)
Deep vermilion, red; compact habit. Late. Medium.

VARIEGATED

The leaves are very similar in colour having ivory/cream edges with green centers.

***P.p.* 'Becky Towe'** (*Mrs June Towe, Shropshire, England. 2000*)
Salmony carmine rose with a darker magenta eye. The spring foliage is bronze tinted. A sport from 'Windsor', raised by a member of the Hardy Plant Society and named after her pet flat-coated retriever dog. Short.

***P.p.* 'Crème de Menthe'**
This plant appears to be the North American version of 'Norah Leigh'.

***P.p.* 'Darwin's Joyce'** (*Witterman & Co. [Darwin Plants], Hillegom, Netherlands. 1995*)
This is synonymous with 'Norah Leigh' but is particularly robust. Late. Medium.

***P.p.* 'Frosted Elegance'**
Pale pink flowers with deep-pink eyes. Leaves are medium green with a narrow cream edge that matures to white. Mid-season. Medium.

P.p. 'Goldmine' (*René van Gaalen, Den Hoorn, Netherlands. 2000*)
Bright cerise flowers. Bred from 'Silvermine', which was a sport from 'Popeye'. Medium.

P.p. 'Harlequin' (*A. Bloom, Bressingham, England. 1959*)
Purple flowers. This is a sport of a very old cultivar, *P.p.* 'Border Gem'
Mid-season. Medium.

P.p. 'Mary Christine'
Salmon-pink with a white eye and flecking. Leaves are variegated cream.
Mid-season. Medium.

P.p. 'Norah Leigh'
White flowers with a mauve eye. Named after Mrs Joan Elliott's mother.
The Elliotts were a well-known family of nurserymen. Medium.

P.p. 'Pink Posie' (*Wendy & Alan Thompson, Guildford, Surrey. 1995*)
Young shoots streaked with pink. The flowers are bright raspberry pink.
Medium.

P.p. 'Rubymine' (*René van Gaalen, Den Hoorn, Netherlands. 2000*)
Red-pink flowers with darker eye. Variegated foliage with cream margins
tinged with red.

P.p. 'Silvermine' (*René van Gaalen, Den Hoorn, Netherlands. 2000*)
White flowers. A sport from 'Popeye'. Medium.

PHLOX MACULATA

This is another excellent border phlox that is sometimes mistaken for
Phlox paniculata but, as the name suggests, it is easily distinguished as its
stems are covered with tiny brown spots. It bears small pink-purple
flowers in cylindrical panicles and its leaves are much glossier, narrower
and a darker green than *P. paniculata*. The lower ones also, usually, stay
in better condition. It comes from the Ohio valley in the USA, extending
to North Carolina and Tennessee but is not found much further south.
In its native habitat it is often found growing along the banks of streams.
It requires similar growing conditions to *P. paniculata* although is happier
on some of the lighter soils and the same propagation methods can be
used. It is not normally susceptible to eelworm. The *maculata* and
carolina cultivars have in recent years been switching back and forth
between to the two species. Here I have followed the listings used in the
current edition of *The RHS Plant Finder*.

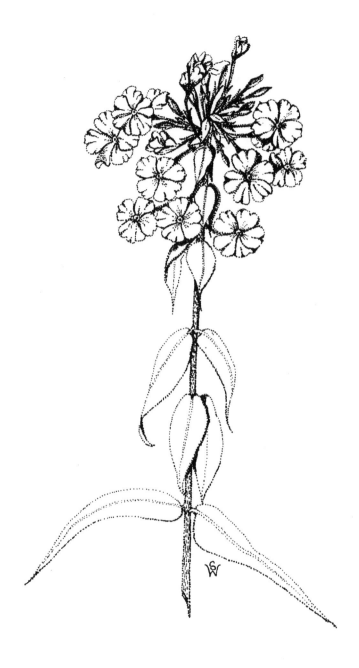

Phlox maculata

Zone 4

Phlox maculata

This is the pink flowered species.

P.m. 'Alpha' (*L.G. Arends, Ronsdorf, Wippertal, Germany. 1918*)

Soft rose-pink. 90cm (3ft).

P.m. 'Delta'

White flowers with a red eye. 75cm (2½ft).

P.m. 'Natascha'

Pink and white striped flowers. This plant is very similar to Van Houtte's famous striped phlox, which was illustrated in Jane London's *The Ladies' Flower-Garden of Ornamental Plants* (1843-44). 90cm (3ft).

P.m. 'Omega' (*Blooms, Bressingham, Norfolk, England. 1960's*)

Near white flowers tinged violet with a pink eye. 90cm (3ft).

P.m. 'Princess Sturdza'

Mauve flowers. Named after a noted French gardener who is one of the leaders in the post-war movement towards informality, diversity and shifting the centre of interest from the design of the grounds to plants.

P.m. 'Rosalinde'

Clear pink. This is an old variety that repeat flowers well. 75cm (2½ft).

P.m. 'Schneelawine' (syn. 'Avalanche')

Pure white flowers. 90cm (3ft).

PHLOX X *ARENDSII*

Georg Arends, of the Rondsorf Nursery in Germany, crossed *Phlox divaricata* and *Phlox paniculata* to create *Phlox* x *arendsii*. These plants have become very scarce in England but have been used for hybridisation on the continent. They are very straggly plants and difficult to establish and keep going but *Phlox* x *arendsii* 'Lisbeth' is the most beautiful pale lilac and worth the struggle. The Jacob Th. De Vroomen nursery in Holland is currently launching a new generation, which is widening the range available.

In the early 1990s Coen Jansen bred a number of phlox hybrids. They all came from open-pollinated plants, the parent being *P. x a.* 'Hilde', which was pollinated by tall, late-flowering plants such as *P. paniculata*, *P.p.* 'Rosa Spier' and *P.p.* 'Lavendelwolke'. The resulting progeny are lovely with a long flowering season. Coen's favourite (and mine) is *P.* 'Utopia', a very tall pale pink, although I think the shorter, white *P.* 'Casablanca' runs it a close second. These were followed in the late 1990s by the Spring Pearl series. These are selected crosses between *P. x arendsii* and a pink cultivar of *P. paniculata*. The new *Phlox x arendsii* and the Spring Pearl series are short, sturdy and designed for use in the front of the border in full sun, although they can be grown in light shade. They are also suitable for containers. If regularly dead-headed they have a long flowering season.

Zone 4

Phlox x arendsii **'Anja'** (*L. G. Arends, Ronsdorf, Wuppertal, Germany. 1960s*) Reddish purple 75cm (2½ft).

P. x a. **'Hilde'** (*L. G. Arends, Ronsdorf, Wuppertal, Germany. 1960s*) Lilac with a pink eye. 75cm (2½ft).

P. x a. **'Lilac Star'** (*Introduced by Jacob Th. de Vroomen, Russell IL, 60075, Netherlands. 2000*) This variety belongs to the new generation *Phlox x arendsii*. They have strong, erect stems. The flowers are lilac-purple with a light, sweet fragrance. The leaves are small, short and dark green. Mid-season. 45cm (18in).

P. x a. **'Lisbeth'** (*L. G. Arends , Ronsdorf, Wuppertal, Germany. 1913*) Pale lilac. 75cm (2½ft).

P. x a. **'Ping Pong'** (*Introduced by Jacob Th. de Vroomen, Russell IL, 60075, Netherlands. 2000*) Another *Phlox x arendsii* belonging to the new generation. Flowers are a soft rose with dark rose eyes that really stand out above the red-green foliage and have a light, sweet fragrance. Stems are also reddish. Mid-season. 45cm (18in).

P. x a **'Rosa Star'** (*Introduced by Jacob Th. de Vroomen, Russell IL, 60075, Netherlands. 2000*) The flowers are soft pink with no other colouring and lightly fragrant. Foliage is dark green. 45cm (18in).

P. x a. **'Sabine'** (*Introduced by Jacob Th. de Vroomen, Russell IL, 60075, Netherlands. 2000*) Bluish-pink flowers above dark green foliage. 50cm (20in).

P. x a. **'Suzanne'** (*L. G. Arends, Ronsdorf, Wuppertal, Germany. 1960s*) White with a red eye. 75cm (2½ft).

SPRING PEARL CULTIVARS

P. **'Miss Jessica'** (*Introduced by Jacob Th. de Vroomen, Russell IL, 60075, Netherlands. 2000*) Lilac-blue flowers fade to white near the centres. Foliage is deep green. This is described as an improved selection from *P.* 'Miss Wilma'. I find the latter an excellent garden plant so it will be interesting to see how *P.* 'Miss Jessica' performs. Short.

P. **'Miss Jill'** (*A. Vershoor & Zoon 1996. Reg No 91*)
Creamy white with small pink eye. Mid-season. 50cm (20in).

P. **'Miss Jo-Ellen'** (*A. Vershoor & Zoon 1996. Reg No 92*)
White with purple-pink blush, dark pink centre. Mid-season. 35cm (14in).

P. **'Miss Karen'** (*A. Vershoor & Zoon 1996. Reg No 93*)
Dark pink with dark red eye. Fragrant. Mid-season. 50cm (20in).

P. **'Miss Margie'** (*A. Vershoor & Zoon. 1996. Reg No 94*)
Lilac-blue. 35cm (14in).

P. **'Miss Mary'**
Clear red flowers with very dark green foliage. 50cm (20in).

P. **'Miss Wilma'**
Lilac flowers fading to white near the centres. This plant is much taller than the others in the Spring Pearl series. Late. 90cm (3ft).

HYBRIDS BRED BY COEN JANSEN

P. **'Casablanca'** (*Coen Jansen, Ankummer Es 15, 7722 RD, Dalfsen, Netherlands. 1990s*)
A very floriferous plant with white star-shaped flowers. Light green leaves. Mid-season. Medium.

P. **'Grace'** (*Coen Jansen, as above*)
White with a red eye. Tall.

P. **'Herfstsering'** (*Coen Jansen, as above*)
Lilac with rose tone and eye. This cultivar is no longer available as Jansen felt it was too prone to mildew. Tall.

P. **'Hesperis'** (*Coen Jansen, as above*)
Lilac-purple flowers in close-packed pyramidal heads. Medium.

P. **'Hortensia'** (*Coen Jansen, as above*)
Pink with a white eye. Tall.

P. **'Luc's Lilac'** (*Coen Jansen, as above*)
Lilac flowers. Tall.

P. **'Matineus'** (*Coen Jansen, as above*)
White with a vivid pink eye. Early.

P. **'Sweet William'** (*Coen Jansen, as above*)
Dark purple, toned pink, with a tiny white eye.

P. **'Utopia'** (*Coen Jansen, as above*)
Pale pink. Vigorous. Late. Tall.

PHLOX DRUMMONDII

Phlox drummondii is an excellent annual phlox. Named after Thomas Drummond, who discovered the plant in Texas and who had led a fairly colourful life. He took over from George Don at the Forfar Nursery in Scotland and in 1825 became assistant naturalist with Sir John Franklin's Arctic expedition. In 1828 he became the first curator of the Belfast Botanic Garden but was dismissed after two and half years. He was somewhat argumentative and had a fatal propensity for strong drink. He then went to Mexico and Texas. In 1831, having promised to forsake fermented liquors for a year, he was sponsored by a number of Botanic Gardens and gardeners, including Dr William Hooker at Glasgow. After undergoing many trials and tribulations plant hunting in the Southern States, he finally went to Cuba in 1835, where he died in unexplained circumstances. This was one of the last plants he sent back.

Phlox drummondii was extensively used in the Victorian period. Seeds should be planted in the spring, either in pots for bedding out in May, or direct into the garden. It also makes a very good and unusual container plant.

Some of the most popular varieties are:

Phlox drummondii 'Chanal'
Double flowers of deep pink. 20cm (8in).

P.d. 'Grandiflora Brilliant'
A very old variety with bright, dark-eyed rose flowers. 45cm (18in).

P.d. 'Mount Hampden'
Semi-double in red, rose, pink, purple, scarlet, and some pastel colours.

P.d. 'Phlox of Sheep'
Varying shades of salmon-pink and apricot. Grows particularly well in containers. 30cm. (1ft).

P.d. 'Tapestry'
Various shades of lilac through to red. Scented. 45cm (18in).

P.d. 'Twinkles'
Mixed colours with star-shaped flowers. 20cm (8in).

Woodland or Shade-loving Species

THESE SPECIES GENERALLY make low mats of prostrate stems, often rooting at the nodes, from which arise upright stems carrying loose heads of flowers in a range of colours from white to deepest pink or blue. They all grow well in partial shade in acid to neutral soils containing abundant humus, which may be leaf-mould, peat, compost or well-rotted manure, and they enjoy plenty of moisture at all times. If the soil is very heavy they will benefit from improved drainage by incorporating coarse grit.

After a few years plants often seem to deteriorate, in which case they should be lifted and split up and replanted after refreshing the soil with plenty of humus and some general fertiliser.

Propagation by means of cuttings of the new growth after flowering is easy, but several species root at the nodes and rooted young plants can be separated and planted. As with so many phlox species seed is not set or can only be found with difficulty, and in any case many of the plants grown are selected forms which are unlikely to come true from seed.

Pests and diseases do not seem to cause many problems in this group, and they are certainly less susceptible to eelworm than the large hybrids

PHLOX ADSURGENS

Phlox adsurgens AGM **Zone 6**
This species from the Pacific Northwest is one of the most beautiful in this group but is generally not quite so strong growing as others. It forms a dense prostrate mat and even in flower is not more than 8cm (3in) high. The opposite leaves are oval to obovate, 2.5cm (1in) long, and the 2cm (¾in) wide flowers in umbels have slightly overlapping petals in the best forms, in a lovely shade of deep salmon pink with a darker pink band down the centre of each petal.

P.a '*Alba*'
An uncommon variety with pure white flowers.

P.a. '*Red Buttes*'
A particularly good form with a well-rounded flower with overlapping petals.

P.a. '*Wagon Wheel*'
This strangely popular cultivar has starry flowers with very narrow parallel-sided petals of similar colour to the type and is possibly a little more vigorous.

Phlox divaricata AGM **Zone 5**

A species from the Eastern States, growing in moist acid to neutral soils, which has been in cultivation since the late 1700s, originally as a lychnis. It is a popular plant for shady gardens. It forms a mat of prostrate stems with broad leaves which root freely at the nodes, and from which upright flowering stems to 30cm (1ft) arise with narrower lanceolate or ovate stem leaves. The flowers are in loose umbels of up to twenty and are individually 2-3cm (¾-1in) wide, usually with notched petals in the type, typically of a good pale violet to lavender colour, but sometimes paler.

The subspecies *P.d.* subsp. *laphamii* occurs to the west of *P. divaricata* on limestone soils in drier areas. The flowers are generally deeper in colour and have un-notched petals in the type, typically of a good violet to lavender colour.

There are a number of cultivars available, differing mainly in colour rather than habit, of which the following are generally available.

P.d. f. ***albiflora***

An uncommon pure white form.

P.d. **'Blue Dreams'**

A tall cultivar with lavender-blue flowers opening from long pointed buds.

P.d. **'Charles Ricardo'**

Is a little paler with a distinct pink eye.

P.d. **'Clouds of Perfume'**

Has pale green lanceolate leaves and large loose heads of extremely pale violet scented flowers with a deeper violet eye.

P.d. **'Dirigo Ice'**

A good vigorous cultivar with palest ice-blue flowers.

P.d. **'Eco Texas Purple'**

Also vigorous with flowering stems up to 35cm (14in) and large loose heads of flowers of a very distinctive deep reddish purple colour.

P.d. **'Fuller's White'**

Is unusual in being clump-forming rather than stoloniferous. It has upright stems of pale green leaves to about 25cm (10in) and fairly dense heads of pure white flowers. It is one of the most popular plants in the garden for slugs and snails, to the extent that in some gardens it is almost ungrowable.

P.d. subsp. ***laphamii*** **'Chattahoochee'** AGM

A selection originally found in Florida by Mrs Norman Henry and is a spectacular garden plant. It makes the usual low mat of stems and the flowering stems are not generally more than 20cm (8in) long. It blooms profusely with luminous lavender flowers with a broad maroon centre. 'Chattahoochee Variegated' is similar but with leaves margined with cream.

P.d. 'Louisiana Purple'
The flowers are a subtle mix of reds and purples.

P.d. 'May Breeze'
A tall cultivar with near-white flowers opening from pale blue buds. The small individual flowers are borne in large loose heads.

P.d. 'Montrose'
Pale lavender-blue flowers. The foliage is variegated, with cream edges. 35cm (14in).

P.d. 'White Perfume'
Is similar to 'Clouds of Perfume' but the petals are pure white.

PHLOX x PROCUMBENS

Phlox x procumbens (Phlox amoena hort.) Zone 5
This is a hybrid between *P. stolonifera* and *P. subulata* and is intermediate in its features, although perhaps favouring the latter in that it is quite compact, but the flower stems are up to 15cm(6in) high. Typically the flowers in dense flat heads are deep purple in colour.

As might be expected from their parentage these plants will grow well in either sun or shade.

P. x p. 'Millstream' AGM
A widely grown cultivar that has pink flowers with a white central zone and a deep pink eye.

P. x p. 'Variegata'
Similar in habit and flower colour to the type but has leaves with an attractive marginal cream variegation.

PHLOX STOLONIFERA

Phlox stolonifera Zone 6
The final species in this group is widely distributed in nature and has been in cultivation since the 18th century. It is similar in habit to *P. divaricata*, making low mats of prostrate stems rooting at the nodes, but the stems and leaves are hairy in this species and the flowering stems are generally shorter to 20-25cm (8-10in), and bear rather lax heads of lavender to violet or white flowers with un-notched petals. There are

several named varieties and all are easily grown in humus-rich soil in partial or full shade. A variegated form is sometimes offered.

Among them the following can be recommended.

P.s. 'Ariane'
An excellent variety with pale green leaves and pure white flowers.

P.s. 'Blue Ridge' AGM
Probably the most popular variety, having been in cultivation for many years. A vigorous carpeter with 20cm (10in) stems of lavender-blue flowers with prominent orange stamens.

P.s. 'Bob's Motley' (*Bob Brown, Cotswold Garden Flowers, Badsey, Worcestershire. 1966*)
Purple flowers with yellow, cream, pink and green variegated leaves. This was a sport from the variegated form of *Phlox stolonifera* with a particularly good colour combination.

P.s 'Fran's Purple'
Flowers a lovely mix of purples, similar in colour to 'Violet Vere' but it is said to be more floriferous.

P.s. 'Home Fires'
A recent introduction with bright pink flowers.

P.s. 'Mary Belle Frey'
Large flowers of a rich raspberry pink..

P.s. 'Pink Ridge'
Very similar to 'Blue Ridge' except in colour, which is a good deep pink.

P.s. 'Sherwood Purple'
Dark purplish-blue flowers. A cultivar that is very popular in the USA and is now becoming available in the UK.

P.s. 'Violet Vere'
Remarkable in having deep violet-purple flowers. Named by Pam Schwerdt after her mother. A plant had been purchased from a florist's shop in Sloane Square but the name could not be traced.

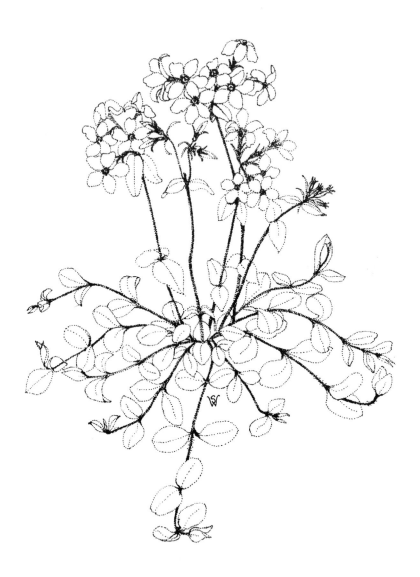

Phlox stolonifera 'Pink Ridge'

Cushion Phlox

THIS GROUP INCLUDES THE SPECIES AND CULTIVARS that are so popular among rock gardeners, easy to grow and very floriferous. They are very undemanding, needing a sunny position and a reasonably well-drained soil. This means that although they are most frequently seen in rock gardens or as wonderful wall plants, there is scope for their use in the front of perennial borders where they will give a colourful display in spring before the main burgeoning of the border in summer.

In general they make low mats or cushions of small needle-like leaves above which appear a mass of solitary flowers or small heads of flowers in spring in a range of colours from white through pink to deep reddish purple and pale to deep lavender.

They can all be propagated from cuttings of the new growths after flowering. Seed is not set freely, but as most of the plants we are dealing with are named cultivars, cuttings are the most suitable method. Generally they are free from diseases.

The following are the commonest and easiest species involved. A few species have been omitted here because they need specialised treatment in the alpine house or scree and are difficult to keep in the garden.

PHLOX BIFIDA

Phlox bifida Zone 5

This species and its cultivars are characterized by a rather looser habit than the other cushion phlox, by longer needle-like leaves and by having flowers with petals deeply notched at the tips, sometimes to half the length of the petal, thus it is often called the Ten Point Phlox. This is a very attractive feature, but it must be said that in general the plants may be a little less robust than others of the group and do best in well-drained soil.

The typical species has deeply notched flowers in shades of lavender blue, sometimes a good clear colour, on mounds about 15cm (6in) high.

P.b. 'Alba'

A variety with pure white flowers, otherwise similar in habit to the type.

P.b. 'Colvin's White'

Another widely available white cultivar. A compact plant with flowers of moderate size with widely spaced deeply notched petals.

P.b. 'Petticoat'

Has pink flowers with darker markings around the eye.

P.b. 'Starbrite'

A taller, looser plant with more rounded flowers with overlapping and more shallowly notched petals, lavender-blue with purple markings around the eye.

A few other cultivars are occasionally seen in catalogues.

PHLOX DIFFUSA

Phlox diffusa (*P. douglasii* var. *diffusa*) **Zone 4**

This is taller and a little looser than most of the forms of *P. douglasii*, making a cushion about 10cm high with abundant flowers, up to three to a stem and 1.5cm wide, lavender, pink, or white, usually with a small white eye, in late spring and early summer. It is not often offered and needs well-drained soil.

PHLOX DOUGLASII

This species is the parent of one of the two main groups of cushion phlox. There is a wealth of cultivars under this name but the same ones may be offered as *P. subulata*, and it seems likely that some at least are of mixed parentage with *P. bifida* also probably involved in those with notched petals.

The type plant from North-West United States makes a dense mat of 1cm (½in) long narrow almost needle-like leaves from which arise stems to 8cm (3in) high with solitary, or less commonly two or three, 1.5cm (¾in) wide flowers with obovate un-notched petals in shades of pink, lavender, or white. The flowers typically sheet the mats so that the leaves are invisible

These plants are invaluable in the garden, easily grown in any soil that is reasonably well drained. They are most commonly used in rock gardens or in walls, where they can be just as effective as aubrieta, but they can add a new dimension with their early flowers to a mixed border, where grit has been incorporated to give better drainage if this is very poor.

Among the many cultivars several have received the Award of Garden Merit, singling them out as reliable and beautiful plants of quality for the garden:

Zone 3

P.d. 'Apollo'

Has large flowers, violet-pink in colour.

P.d. 'Boothman's Variety' AGM

An old favourite, lilac-blue with a darker blue centre.

44

P. d. 'Concorde'
Has deep reddish-purple flowers with a pale eye.

P.d. 'Crackerjack' AGM
A more recent introduction with masses of deep magenta flowers.

P.d. 'Eva'
One of the more compact-growing cultivars with lavender flowers.

P.d. 'Iceberg' AGM
A very good white with the faintest flush of violet.

P.d. 'Lilakönigin' (Lilac Queen)
A very vigorous cultivar with white flowers with a palest violet tinge.

P.d 'Red Admiral' AGM
Another very worthy recipient of the AGM with deep red flowers.

P.d. 'Rose Cushion'
A very compact plant with an abundance of pink flowers

P.d. 'Rosea'
An old variety with rose-pink flowers

P.d. 'Violet Queen'
Another compact cultivar with deep violet flowers

P.d. 'Waterloo'
A rather loose-growing plant with very dark reddish-violet flowers

A search through specialised catalogues will produce several other names and descriptions.

PHLOX NIVALIS

Phlox nivalis Zone 7
This is a small mat-forming plant, slower-growing that *P. subulata* or *P. douglasii*, with similar narrow leaves to these and usually with mid-pink flowers although they can be almost white or a deeper purplish pink. It has two good compact cultivars worth growing in well-drained soil:

P.n. 'Camlaensis'
Stronger growing with pale salmon-pink flowers.

P.n. 'Nivea'
A little more compact and the flowers are pure white.

PHLOX SUBULATA

Phlox subulata Zone 5
This is the most popular and widely grown group of Cushion Phlox, and differs very little from *P. douglasii*, which is described above and is native

to the North West of the United States. *P. subulata* is widely distributed through North East America, where an enormous range of different colour forms are found, from which the earlier cultivars are probably derived. In addition to the variation in flower colour there is also a considerable variety in compactness, height and length of leaf.

The cultivars all form low mats of needle-like leaves, smothered in flowers in spring. The colour range is large from white to red to deepest violet and the flowers differ in the degree of overlap of the petals and the notching of their tips. They are easily grown, as long as the soil is reasonably well drained, and all benefit from being cut back after flowering to prevent them becoming straggly.

P.s. **'Alexander's Surprise'** Large rose-pink. Vigorous.

P.s. **'Amazing Grace'** White with a deep pink eye.

P.s. **'Apple Blossom'** Deep pink. Very compact.

P.s. **'Atropurpurea'** Reddish-purple. Quick-growing.

P.s. **'Betty'** Pink with darker basal spots. Loose-growing.

P.s. **'Bonita'** Large purplish-pink.

P.s. **'Brilliant'** Rose pink. Large mats.

P.s. **'Candy Stripe'** See P.s. 'Tamaongalei'

P.s. subsp. ***brittonii*** **'Rosea'** Pink .

P.s. **'Daisy Hill'** Deep pink with a darker eye.

P.s. **'Fairy'** Pale violet with dark basal spots.

P.s. **'Greencourt Purple'** Purplish pink with dark eye.

P.s. **'Kelly's Eye'** AGM. Pale pink with dark eye. Very flat mat.

P.s. **'Lavinia'** White with violet spot. Prostrate.

P.s. **'Lilacina'** (syn. 'G.F. Wilson') Pale lilac with a few dark spots.

P.s. **'Maischnee'** (May Snow) Pure white overlapping petals.

P.s. **'Marjorie'** Pinkish lavender. Prostrate.

P.s. **'McDaniel's Cushion'** Deep rose, broad petals. Vigorous.

P.s. **'Nettleton Variation'** Pale pink. Well-variegated leaves.

P.s. **'Oakington Blue Eyes'** (syn. 'Blue Eyes') Deep lavender. Vigorous.

P.s. **'Red Wings'** AGM. Pinkish red with a dark eye. Vigorous.

P.s. **'Ronsdorfer Schöne'** (Beauty of Ronsdorf) Pinkish-lavender with dark violet basal spots. Very low and compact.

P.s. **'Samson'** Large, salmon-pink, red eye.

P.s. **'Scarlet Flame'** Large carmine.

P.s. **'Tamaongalei'** White striped with deep pink. A good recent arrival.

P.s. **'Temiskaming'** Vivid magenta. A good old favourite.

P.s. **'White Delight'** Pure white. Vigorous.

P.s. **'Vivid'** Deep salmon-pink. Compact.

Some other species

THERE ARE TWO OR THREE OTHER SPECIES intermediate in height between the cushions and mats described earlier and the large border plants. These are excellent in mixed borders in rich moist soil, and will tolerate a certain amount of shade if necessary. All are easily propagated from cuttings of young growth in early summer or by division. They are generally free from disease but may be subject to the same troubles as the large cultivars.

PHLOX CAROLINA

Phlox carolina is found throughout North Carolina and south eastern United States. In its natural habitat it has a low water requirement. Its upright stems have showy clusters of flowers in late spring and early summer. The species itself is rarely offered but some of the cultivars are excellent, freely available plants for the front or middle of the border, usually about 40-50cm (16-20in) high when in flower. All are clump-forming with glossy lanceolate leaves on upright to procumbent stems, and large heads of 2cm(¾ in) wide flowers.

Zone 6

P.c. angusta
A light, airy plant with rose-violet flowers. 45cm (18in).

P.c. 'Bill Baker'
Has spreading stems and masses of deep pink flowers with a paler centre. In the early 1980s Bill Baker, who was an HPS member, was on holiday in New England. He was taken by Professor Deno to see some of the local wild flowers and Bill saw this phlox growing in a wood. He photographed it and as the professor had a patch in his garden he provided Bill with seed. Whilst the plant was being identified by various authorities in England it became known as 'Bill Baker'. It has had a number of name changes but in 1990 it was registered by Joe Sharman as *Phlox carolina* 'Bill Baker'. 50cm (20in).

P.c. 'Magnificence'
Upright plant with narrower trusses of pink-mauve flowers.90cm (3ft).

P.c 'Reine du Jour'
White with a maroon eye. 75cm (2½ft.)

P.c. 'Miss Lingard' AGM
White flowers. An old cultivar dating back to the early 20th century and

48

bred by Mr. Lingard, an amateur gardener. In the United States its common name is the wedding phlox. It is a tall, upright plant with lovely glossy foliage. 90cm (3ft).

PHLOX PILOSA

This species is not seen so often in gardens but resembles *P. carolina* in habit with lanceolate leaves and spreading stems and abundant pink flowers with a white eye in early summer, continuing for several weeks.
Zone 5

HARDINESS ZONES

Zone 3	-40 to -34° C
Zone 4	-34 to -29° C
Zone 5	-29 to -23° C
Zone 6	-23 to -18° C
Zone 7	-18 to -12° C
Zone 8	-12 to -7° C
Zone 9	-7 to -1° C

Further Reading

Coats, Alice. *Flowers and their Histories.* 1967.

Coats, Alice. *The Book of Flowers.* 1974.

Coats, Peter. *Flowers.* 1970.

Douglas, James. *Hardy Florists Flowers.* 1880.

Fisher, John. *The Origins of Garden Plants.* 1982.

Fox Wilson, G. RHS Journal 49. 1924.

Fuchs, Herman, *Phlox Stauden und Polsterphloxe.* 1994.

Kennedy, John, *Page's Prodromus; Nomenclature of all the plants, indigenous and exotic cultivated in the Southampton Botanic Gardens,* 1817.

Leighton, Anne. *American Gardens in the Eighteenth Century.* 1976.

Loudon, J.C. *Encyclopaedia of Plants,* 1829.

Loudon, Jane. *Ornamental Flowers.* Classic Natural History Prints. 1991.

Nypels. *Annales de la Society Belge de Micro* xxiii. 1898.

Symons-Jeune, B.H.B. *Phlox,* Garden Book Club. 1954.

Wherry, Edgar T. *The Genus Phlox,* 1955.

The Hardy Plant Vol. 2 No.1, Obituary of Capt, B.H.B. Symons, 1959.

Where to buy Phlox

UNITED KINGDOM
Beeches Nursery
Village Centre, Ashdon, Saffron Walden, Essex CB1O 2HB
Blackmore & Langdon Ltd
Pensford, Bristol, Avon BS39 4JL
Chiltern Seeds
Bortree Stile, Ulverston, Cumbria LA12 7PB
Cotswold Garden Flowers
Sands Lane, Badsey, Evesham, Worcestershire WR11 6EZ
Four Seasons
Forncett St Mary, Norwich, Norfolk NR16 1JT
Green Farm Plants
Bury Court, Bentley, Farnham, Surrey GU10 5LZ
Hillview Hardy Plants
Worfield, Nr Bridgnorth, Shropshire WV15 5NT
Rumsey Gardens
117 Drift Road, Clanfield, Waterlooville, Hampshire PO8 0PD
Thompson & Morgan
Poplar Lane, Ipswich, Suffolk IP8 3BU

NETHERLANDS
Hans Kramer
Kwekerij de Hessenhof, Hessenweg 41, 6718 TC Ede
De Kleine Plantage
Handerweg 1, 9967 TC Eenrum
Kwekerij Oudolf
Broekstraat 17, 6999 DE Hummelo,
Th. Ploeger en Zn BV
Blauwkapelseweg 73, 3731 EB De Bilt,

GERMANY
Foerster-Stauden GmbH
Am Raubfang 6, 14469 Potsdam-Bornim
StaudengaertnereiKlose
Rosenstrasse 10, D -34253, Lohfelden -Kessel
Peter und Bärbel zur Linden
49143 Bissendorf, Linner Kirchweg 2, Linne

Stefan Rank & Ulrike zur Linden
Gartebstr 13, 82279 Eching am Ammersee

THE UNITED STATES
Heronswood Nursery Ltd
7530 NE 288th Street, Kingston, WA 98346-502
We-Du Nurseries
2055 Polly Spout Road, Marion, North Carolina 28752
White Flower Farm
Litchfield, Connecticut 06759-0050

NEW ZEALAND
Peak Perennials
27 Troop Street, Havelock North
Marshwood Gardens & Nursery
Leonard Road, West Plains, RD4 Invercargill

JAPAN
Miyoshi Perennials
3181 Takeahara, Kamisasao, Kitakoma-gun, Yamanashi 408-0041

Websites: *The Hardy Plant Society:* www.hardy-plant.org.uk
For Websites of individual nurseries see *The RHS Plant Finder*

ACKNOWLEDGEMENTS

We are greatly indebted to Jane Sterndale-Bennett and Sue Ward, without whose unfailing support and encouragement this booklet would not have been written. We would also like to acknowledge the help given to us by Tony Lord and, in Holland, by Coen Jansen, the Jacob de Vroomen Nursery and René van Gaalen.